Selkie

by
LAURIE BROOKS GOLLOBIN

Copyright 1997
Anchorage Press, Inc.
Post Office Box 8067
New Orleans, Louisiana 70182

ISBN 0-87602-353-7

SELKIE is the first play to be honored in the same year by both the National Waldo M. and Grace C. Bonderman Youth Theatre Playwriting Workshop at IUPUI, and the Youth Theatre Playwriting Symposium in Indianapolis - - and the New Visions/New Voices forum for Plays-in-Progress for Young Audiences at the John F. Kennedy Center in Washington, D.C. Both events occurred in 1995.

Cover Art by Boswell Williams

Selkie was given its first rehearsed reading at New York University's Black Box Theatre, produced by the Program in Educational Theatre, February 24th and 25th, with the following cast:

CAST

Pa	John Doerner
Margaret	Joan Ritchey
Duncan	Matthew Zahner
Ellen Jean	Allison Hedges
Tam	John Fuller
Black-Haired Selkie	Robin Sheuer
Red-Haired Selkie	Paula Heitman
Voice of Stage Directions	Julia Perloski

PRODUCTION STAFF

Author	Laurie Brooks Gollobin
Producer	Frans Rijunbout
Director	Nancy Swortzell
Stage Manager	Julia Perlowski
Asst. Stage Manager	Shiang-Tsz Liou
Set Advisor	Roger Hanna
Sound Operator	Cathryn Clarke
Lighting Designer	Jason Livingston
Lightboard Operator	Vinnie Zeoli

Selkie was a winner of the sixth National Waldo M. and Grace C.
Bonderman Youth Theatre Playwriting Workshop sponsored by Indiana
University-Purdue University at Indianapolis and was featured in a
rehearsed reading at the 1995 Youth Theatre Playwriting Symposium
held in Indianapolis. The reading, held on March 31st, at Indiana Reper-
tory Theatre, featured the following cast:

Selkie

Playwright: Laurie Brooks Gollobin
Director: Amie Brockway
Dramaturg: Lauren Friesen
Response Leader: Suzan Zeder

IRT Upperstage

Pa: Richard Henson
Margaret: Lynne Perkins
Ellen Jean: Bernadette Perez
Duncan: Will Gould
Tam: Bill Simmons
Black Hair: Suzi Moore Fenton
Red Hair: Stephanie Kern
Stage Directions: Sandra Hartlieb

Selkie was also featured in a rehearsed reading at the 1995 New Vi-
sions/New Voices: A Forum for Plays-in-Progress for Young Audiences,
at the John F. Kennedy Center in Washington, D.C.

Saturday, May 20, 3:00 PM
Theatre Lab

Selkie

Commissioned by New York University Program in Educational Theatre

Playwright: Laurie Brooks Gollobin
Director: Nancy Swortzell
Stage Manager: Linda Marvel*

CAST
(* denotes member of Actors Equity)

Pa:	Lawrence Redmond*
Margaret:	Tia Howell*
Ellen Jean:	April Cantor
Duncan:	Stephen F. Schmidt*
Tam:	Randy Howk
Black Hair:	Becky Woodley*
Red Hair:	Elizabeth van den Berg*

Selkie premiered at The Frederick Loewe Theatre, produced by New York University's Program in Educational Theatre, March 22, 1996.

The School of Education
New York University
The Department of Music and Performing Arts Professions
The Program in Educational Theatre

present

The World-Premiere Production of the Prize-Winning Play

Selkie

by
Laurie Brooks Gollobin

Directed by
Nancy Foell Swortzell

Setting Designed by
Roger Hanna

Lighting Design by
Jason Livingston

Costumes Designed by
Michele Wynne

Original Music by
Carlos Guedes

Choreography by
Hye Jueng Chung

Stage Manager
Amy Koblensky

CAST
(in order of appearance)

Pa	John Doerner
Margaret	Ann McCormack*
Ellen Jean	Karen Cooke
Duncan	Mathew Zahner
Tam	Aubrey Chamberlin
Black Haired Selkie	Maria Goldstein
Red Haired Selkie	Maria Papageorgioe

Dedicated to the memories of **my mother**,
who loved stories,
and
Aurand Harris,
who loved the little girl with the webbed hands.

SELKIE

CHARACTERS

Pa:	Duncan's father, a fisherman.
Margaret:	Late twenties, lovely and pale skinned, with brown hair.
Ellen Jean:	Brown-haired daughter of Duncan and Margaret, thirteen years old. Has webbed hands.
Duncan:	A crofter. Early thirties.
Tam:	A traveller (gypsy) lad of fourteen, with black eyes and a keen sense of mischief.
Black Hair:	One of the selkie-folk women with long, black hair.
Red Hair:	One of the selkie-folk women with long, red hair.

TIME

One hundred years ago, on Midsummer's Eve (June 21st) when the people of Orkney herald the coming of summer with a celebration called the Johnsmas Foy. They call this time the simmer dim, when there is daylight even at midnight.

SETTING:

The Orkney Islands north of the wild, rocky coast of Scotland. The stage is set to suggest the rocky seacoast. There is a large flat rock at center. Downstage of the rock, rippling lights create the sea. The upstage perimeter of the stage is dotted with rocks and grass.

A movable set piece defines the interior of a crofthouse (Orkney farm-house). There are two small windows with shutters upstage. In the center of the crofthouse is a peat fire, which is burned down to glowing embers. There are two, low stools standing around the fire and a wooden rocking chair. There are two doors leading to other areas of the crofthouse and one leading to the outdoors.

SELKIE

*(Fiddle music. Dim daylight. The Beach. It is
Midsummer's Eve, when there is light for twenty hours a
day. Pa is downstage, playing his fiddle. He is scruffy
and bearded, with a kind voice and warm ways.*

*Through the thick fog, called "the har", a large flat rock
can be seen at center. Rippling lights create the sea
downstage of the rock. Sounds of the wind and the sea.
The sounds of the selkies singing in the distance. Pa
tucks his fiddle under his arm.)*

PA: There was alus the sound of the sea *(He imitates)* and
the sound of the wind *(He imitates)*. Aye, and the
selkies singing. *(He imitates the selkies.)*

*(Duncan, as a young man of about eighteen, enters,
carrying a rake and a bag for gathering seaweed.)*

There was also a young crofter named Duncan who
lived by the sea. Through the thick fog he could see
them approachin' the rocks - the selkie folk - seals that
live in the water, but change into humans one magical
night each year. It was that night . . . Midsummer's Eve,
the night o' the grand celebration called the Johnsmas
Foy.

*(Three selkies, Black Hair, Red Hair and a brown
spotted selkie enter and move in the sea area toward the
rock at center. Duncan hides himself behind upstage
rocks. The selkies emerge onto the rock at center.)*

He'd heard the stories told round the peat fires of the
grey seals that shed their pelts and become beautiful
lasses, but he niver believed them. Yet here, before his
own eyes were three selkies on the shore and as he
watched, they shed their skins.

(Selkie music. Joyously, the three throw off their skins and are transformed into beautiful young women; one red-haired, one black-haired, and one brown-haired.)

PA: One was a fair lass with golden-red hair, another young lass with shinin', black hair, and last . . . the fairest lass he had ever seen, with brown hair shimmerin' in the dim northern lights.

(As the music soars into the night, the selkie girls leap off the rock and do a wild dance on the beach as Duncan watches unseen in the shadows.)

They danced, the three selkie lasses, danced on the land, like waves on the sea. As he watched them leap wildly aboot the beach, he looked at the brown-haired selkie lass with all the eyes in his head. A strange feelin' came over him, a powerful feelin'. He knew he must take her, the brown-haired selkie lass, take her home tae be his sea wife. Yes, and he knew he must steal her pelt, like in the stories. Withoot her pelt, she could niver go back tae the sea, but must follow him wherever he might lead her.

(Duncan comes out of his hiding place and approaches the women. The black-haired girl sees him and cries out a warning to the others. The selkie folk grab their pelts and enter the sea area. Duncan runs forward and takes up the pelt of the brown-haired girl. She reaches out her arms, imploring him to give back her pelt. Duncan firmly tucks the pelt underneath his arm. The girl slowly collapses on the beach, crying bitterly. Duncan offers his hand to the selkie girl. She hesitates. Duncan takes her hand, kisses it, and never taking his eyes from her face, leads her offstage.)

'Tis true. It happened. The crofter was my son, Duncan, and because she wouldna say her name, we called his sea-wife Margaret. Their only bairn, a daughter - was named Ellen Jean.

(Ellen Jean enters and runs forward onto the rock at center. She gazes out to sea as if looking for something, then swiftly enters the water and exits.)

(Lights fade on beach and come up on the interior of the crofthouse. Margaret sits on a stool, winding wool, working the yarn carefully between her fingers. She is much changed from when we saw her in the first scene. Her body is bent and she wears a shapeless homespun dress with an apron. She moves with an odd, shuffling gait, as though her limbs are too heavy for her body.)

(Pa begins to play a lively tune on his fiddle. He enters the crofthouse, fiddling, as Ellen Jean enters and begins to dance about the room. The dancing is similar to the dancing performed by the three selkies in the first scene. Ellen Jean's long, brown hair swings about her as she dances. She wears a nondescript homespun dress tied at the waist, with unusually long sleeves which hang down, covering her hands. She shouts for punctuation as she dances. Pa ends the tune as Ellen Jean leaps into the air and lands gracefully on the floor in a heap.)

PA: *(Laughing)* Well done, bonny lass! There's none can dance the music tae life as yerself.

MARGARET: Aye. She's the gift in her, our Ellen Jean.

ELLEN JEAN: Tis no' guid yet, fer all the tryin'.

PA: It'll come tae ye, in time, if ye wait.

ELLEN JEAN: Waitin' fer this, waitin' fer that. When will all the waitin' be over?

PA: When ye're stone dead, buried in the ground, and cold as the fishes.

MARGARET: Then ye're wishin' ye had the waitin' tae do.

ELLEN JEAN: Sometimes I have the strangest feelin', walkin' through
                 the days sleepin' like. One day I'll wake up an'
                 everything'll be different.

PA: Different? Worse is more likely.

ELLEN JEAN: Oh, Pa, ye canno' tell the future. Mither, will ye do up
                 me hair? It always comes all far-flunglike when I'm
                 dancin' wild.

MARGARET: *(Smiling)* A fine nest fer the birds ye have there.

                 *(Margaret combs Ellen Jean's hair, fastening it with a
                 clasp.)*

                 Song: *(Sung a Capella by Margaret.)*

                 Listen to the Sea
                      Music by Elliot Sokolov
                      Lyrics by Laurie Brooks Gollobin

                 Voices whisper with the wind
                 Of places ye have niver been.
                 Singin' songs of ebb and flow
                 Of secrets ye will someday know.

                 Listen tae the sea
                 There is a land far beneath
                 Awaken from yer sleep
                 Tae the mysteries doon below.

                 Selkies glidin' inbetween
                 Tides that play upon the sea
                 Callin' ye tae come along
                 Beckon ye tae sing the song.

Listen tae the sea
There is a land far beneath
Awaken from yer sleep
Tae the mysteries doon below.

ELLEN JEAN: Thank ye, Mither, ye alus do it best.

(Margaret kisses Ellen Jean's forehead.)

MARGARET: Eyes green as the sea.

PA: A brown-haired lass, there's none so fair,
Neither golden nor black locks can compare.

ELLEN JEAN: Dunna be sayin' that. Ye're only feelin' sorry fer me.

PA: I like rhymin' is all.
Eetam, peetam, penny pie, Pop-a-larum, jinkam jie,
Stand thoo there til I come by.

(Angrily, Ellen Jean starts to leave.)

Dunna be goin' off in a huff! What's got ye so ill-bisted?

ELLEN JEAN: I canna abide rhymin' is all.

PA: I meant ye no disrespect.

ELLEN JEAN: Day after day I got tae hear the others sayin' hateful rhymes aboot me.

PA: What a bulder o' nonsense! Dunna be payin' attention tae what the others say. It's the inside o' ye that matters.

ELLEN JEAN: No one wants to know me inside, they're too busy gawkin' at the outside.

MARGARET: People's afraid o' what's different, fearin' what they dunna understand.

ELLEN JEAN: None o' them others wants tae be wi' me.

PA: I do.

ELLEN JEAN: I dunna care fer that.

PA: Dunna care fer yer old Grandpa?

              (He takes a stance like a puffin, and waddles about the room, making the high-pitched "hey-al" sound of the puffin breed. Ellen Jean scowls.)

              I remember when 'at sent ye rollin' on the floor wi' laughin'.

ELLEN JEAN: When I was a bairn.

PA: How aboot this?

              (He configures his body to imitate a sheep and makes ridiculous bleeting sounds.)

ELLEN JEAN: Ye've gone daft.

PA: *(Physicalizing himself into a cat. Cat voice.)* Rrrrrrrrrrrr. Meow. Skim off the cream fer me dinner, I'm a peedie bit hungry.

              (Pa rubs his shoulder up against her, knocking her down. Ellen Jean laughs.)

              There. I've made ye laugh.

ELLEN JEAN: Pa, ye're me family. Ye've no choice but tae be with me.

PA: Buy, buy, that's no way tae talk.

ELLEN JEAN: It's the others - I wish the others liked me.

MARGARET: The lads and lasses'll take notice when they see yer
              dancin' at the Foy this night.

PA: It'll be a celebration like none afore it. The torches
              o'heather cracklin'. The dancin' and singin' til dawn. I
              can see the looks on em'. Eyes wide as saucers with
              the surprise.

              (Ellen Jean hangs her head and is silent.)

              (Pa imitates village voices.) Look! Have ye niver seen
              the like o' the dancin'! More wonderous than the skelly
              sun hittin' the cliffs o' Hoy! Who is she, 'at bonnie lass?

ELLEN JEAN: I'll no' be dancin' at the Foy.

PA: Ye're thirteen. Yer fither expects ye tae dance. He's
              bragged aboot it from Kirkwall tae Stromness.

MARGARET: *(Caressing Ellen Jean's hair)* Yer dancin' is a gift. Ye
              must no' hide what is worthy in yerself. Perhaps when
              the others see 'at side o' ye . . .

ELLEN JEAN: They'll hate the dancin' and think me a fool!

              *(Ellen Jean turns in anger and charges for the door. The
              door opens and Duncan enters. Duncan is tall and dark-
              haired; a lanky, awkward man who looks as though he
              isn't quite comfortable in his skin.)*

DUNCAN: *(Stopping Ellen Jean at the door.)* Hover ye noo, lass.
              What's yer hurry?

ELLEN JEAN: No hurry, Fither.

DUNCAN: Sit ye doon then. I'd be havin' a word wi' ye.

              (Duncan goes to Margaret and kisses her lovingly.)

DUNCAN: Pale as the winter sky and twice as lovely.

                  (Ellen Jean tries to slip out of the room unnoticed.)

MARGARET: A lie is harder tae tell in the long haul than the hardest
                  truth.

PA: The truth! There's a slippery fish, just when ye 've
                  caught it up, it slides away from ye.

DUNCAN: Tae me ye're bonny as ever. Workin' each day I'm only
                  waitin' fer evenin' tae be home with ye . . . and Jean.
                  (Duncan spots Ellen Jean leaving.)

                  Jean! Come hither, Lass. James Leslie saw ye yester-
                  day swimmin' oot beyond the voe. Ellen Jean, I've told
                  ye and told ye no' tae swim oot beyond the voe. Even
                  the finest swimmer in Orkney must respect the tides.
                  They change in a peedie minute and pull the strongest
                  swimmer doon into the blackness.

ELLEN JEAN: I know the tides.

DUNCAN: Then why do ye swim oot beyond the voe? Is it a watery
                  grave ye'd be after?

ELLEN JEAN: I canno' help meself. Somethin' pulls me doon tae the
                  beach and in tae the sea.

DUNCAN: I'll no' have ye riskin' yer life when the har rolls in and ye
                  canna see beyond yer nose. None o' the others would
                  dare swim in these waters. I dunna understand. Why
                  do ye no' stay on land with the others?

ELLEN JEAN: I had tae swim oot tae the skerrie.

DUNCAN: What were ye thinkin', Lass? At's near two miles oot tae
                  sea.

MARGARET: 'Twas the selkies callin'. The red and the black.

ELLEN JEAN: They came back, Mither, just as ye said they would.

MARGARET: Aye, at Midsummer's tide.

ELLEN JEAN: One red as the sun goin' down, the other dark as peat.

ELLEN JEAN: Noses lifted straight oot o' the water, like they'us lookin'
              fer somethin'.

(Margaret looks toward the sea.)

DUNCAN: There are hundreds o' selkies swimmin' in these waters,
              alike as one another.

ELLEN JEAN: I knowed 'em straight away and no mistake. I saw their
              eyes up closelike. Human eyes, they were. They'us
              cryin'.

DUNCAN: Ach, 'twas only sea water drippin'.

MARGARET: Selkies cry just as humans do. And fer the same
              reasons. Longin' fer what's been lost and canno' be
              found.

ELLEN JEAN: They'us callin' me. They wanted me tae follow 'em.

DUNCAN: I'll no' ask ye tae explain it. Just no' tae do it.

ELLEN JEAN: I try tae stay on land, Fither, but then I'm achin' fer the
              feel o' the water and the pull o' the waves.

*(Ellen Jean moves her arms to illustrate her thoughts
and her long sleeves fall back to reveal her hands. The
crofthouse grows silent as Ellen Jean realizes she has
shown her hands to her father. She instinctively hides
them behind her back.)*

DUNCAN: Sha' me yer hands.

PA: Giddy God, noo ye've done it.

MARGARET: Duncan, come have yer ale. Its waitin'.

PA: Aye. I'm thirsty as a landlocked fisherman.

MARGARET: I've fresh baked bannock. Ye must be hungry.

DUNCAN: *(To Margaret)* I'll no' be dissuaded. I'm waitin', Lass.

               (Ellen Jean slowly holds out her hands for Duncan.)

               Webbed, they have grown webbed again. Where's me
               gully knife?

               *(Duncan pulls the knife out of the back of his belt and,
               using his belt, sharpens it with a stropping motion.)*

MARGARET: They'll only grow back, like alus.

PA: Leave her hands alone, won't ye? There's naught tae
               be done fer it.

MARGARET: Aye. Tis no guid tae cut 'em.

ELLEN JEAN: *(Bravely)* It doesna' hurt too much, Mither.

               (Pa gets up and reaches for his coat.)

PA: 'At pony'll be wantin' tae be fed.

MARGARET: Dunna run from it, Pa. Help me.

PA: Dunna cut her, man. There's naught tae be done fer it.

MARGARET: Even if ye cut 'em clean off, she'll niver be like the
               others.

DUNCAN: Who will she be like, then? She's thirteen now, time tae
               think o' makin' a guid marriage to a crofter with land,
               home and hearth. She'll need more than a dowry tae
               fetch a husband.

MARGARET: Let the future be takin' care o' itself.

DUNCAN: Ye'd have me do nothin'! I canna bear tae hear the
               others laugh and make sport o' her. I wilna' stand idle,
               seein' her married off tae some tinker like that dirty Tam
               McCodrun withoot a sturdy tub fer washin' or a strip o'
               land tae keep his family fed.

MARGARET: I've heard tell o' him who took a stunder tae love a lass
               wi' naught but hersel' tae offer.

ELLEN JEAN: Cut them, fither. I want tae be like the others.

               (Ellen Jean obediently lays her hands on the table.)

DUNCAN: 'At's a good lass. Hold yer hands steady.

               *(Ellen Jean turns her head away. Duncan positions the
               knife to cut the first web. Margaret rushes forward and
               stops Duncan.)*

MARGARET: No! Cuttin' her hands wilna keep her from the sea! Ye
               canno' shape her intae yer dreams o' what's tae come or
               cut her tae fit ye like a bit o' cloth. Look at her! Do ye
               no' see she's bonny as she is?

               *(Duncan drops the knife as Margaret sobs. He gathers
               Margaret into his arms.)*

DUNCAN: There, there, darlin'. Dunna cry. I canna' bear tae hear
               ye cry. I'll no' cut 'em. I'll no' cut 'em.

               (Ellen Jean quietly picks up the knife.)

PA: Ellen Jean, go oot tae the byre. 'At pony wants feedin'.

                   (Ellen Jean looks toward her parents and hesitates.)

ELLEN JEAN: Then I'll cut them meself!

                   (Ellen Jean slashes the largest web. She cries out and drops the knife, holding her cut hand high in the air.)

BLACKOUT.

                   (Dim daylight. The beach. Sounds of the sea and the wind. Sounds of the selkies. Ellen Jean sits on the rock at center, looking out to sea. Enter Tam. He wears dirty trousers, dingy white shirt and a faded vest that might once have been colorful. His hair hangs long and stringy, falling often and annoyingly into his eyes. His face, hands and bare feet are streaked with dirt and he carries a tin pail. Tam begins to dig for limpets, then sees Ellen Jean.)

TAM: Look what the sea washed up on the beach. A young bit o' skirly-wheeter.

ELLEN JEAN: Go away and dunna daive me with yer gabbin'.

TAM: I warn ye once, I warn ye twice,
                   I warn ye oot the glowrie's eyes.

ELLEN JEAN: Stop 'at! Stop sayin' 'at hateful rhyme!

                   (Ellen Jean puts her hands covered by her long sleeves over her ears to block out the sounds.)

TAM: Hie thee Lass 'at swims in the sea,
                   Stay away from thee and me!

                   (Ellen Jean ignores him. He laughs.)

TAM: What're ye doin' here? Waitin' fer the King o' the sea
                tae come courtin' ye?

ELLEN JEAN: If he wus, ye'd likely bash in his head with a club, skin
                'im alive on the beach an' sell his pelt.

TAM: Fetch a pretty penny, too, more'n likely.

ELLEN JEAN: Ye're an evil lad, I saw ye doon on the skerrie yesterday
                ballin' stones at the selkies.

TAM: Aye, me and the lads. Missed 'em clean away, too.
                More's the pity.

ELLEN JEAN: How can ye be so cruel tae harmless creatures?

TAM: Harmless! Witches they are. Condemned fer their sins
                tae live in the sea.

ELLEN JEAN: That's no' true.

TAM: Eatin' up the herrin' an' starvin' honest fishin' folk.

ELLEN JEAN: The selkies have a right tae eat as much as any crea-
                ture.

TAM: (Mysteriously) Comin' up on the land tae steal the
                peedie bairns from their mithers, just like the trolls.

ELLEN JEAN: That's a lie! The selkies have done naught but
                kindnesses fer folk, savin' 'em from drownin' and the
                like.

TAM: Ye like the selkies so much, why dunna ye go live in the
                sea with 'em!

                (Ellen Jean is silent.)

                Cat got yer tongue, Selkie Lass? Got nuthin' tae say?

ELLEN JEAN: Nuthin' tae say tae the likes o' thee.

               *(Tam lifts a handful of Ellen Jean's hair and flips it
               playfully.)*

ELLEN JEAN: *(Recoiling)* Dunna touch me.

TAM: *(Becoming aware of his dirty hands.)* Ye'd think I had
               the pox, instead o' a bit o' honest dirt.

ELLEN JEAN: Honest dirt washes off. It's the dirty inside I'm thinkin' of.

TAM: Miss high and mighty. Stickin' yer nose up, keepin'
               away from me like I'm lower 'an sheep filth. Because yer
               fither's got a bit o' land and a byre doesna' make ye so
               grand.

ELLEN JEAN: I didna say 'at.

TAM: Ye hate me because I'm a traveller, don't ye. A
               wanderin' gypsy withoot a home. Ye're like all the
               others.

ELLEN JEAN: I'm no' like the others.

TAM: Get off this beach and leave me tae gather me limpets
               fer supper.

               *(Tam begins to forage among the rocks for limpets to fill
               his pail.)*

ELLEN JEAN: I have a right tae be here.

TAM: Get off, I said.

ELLEN JEAN: No. I wilna be bullied aboot.

TAM: *(Threateningly)* Get off afore I run ye off . . . or worse!

ELLEN JEAN: I'll no' give in tae the likes o' thee, Dirty Tam McCodrun!

(Tam runs to Ellen Jean, grabs her by her upraised wrists and shakes her.)

TAM: Dunna call me 'at! Dunna ever call me 'at!

ELLEN JEAN: Let me go! Let me go!

(In the struggle Tam loses his footing and nearly falls into the sea. Ellen Jean instinctively reaches out and grabs Tam to save him from falling. For a moment it looks as though they will both fall, then they regain their balance. Tam looks down at her hands. The long sleeves of her dress have fallen back to reveal her bloody fingers. Ellen Jean breaks free of Tam's grasp and cradles her hurt hand.)

TAM: *(Looking at his hands.)* Blood! Ye're hurt! Damn me ill-bisted temper!

ELLEN JEAN: Hie thee away from me!

TAM: I didna mean tae hurt ye, only ye called me . . . that name. No one calls me Dirty Tam tae me face.

ELLEN JEAN: Tis none o' yer doin'.

TAM: How did ye hurt yer hand then?

ELLEN JEAN: 'Tis nothin'. An accident.

TAM: A bad one, by the looks o' it.

ELLEN JEAN: A slip o' the hand is all.

(Tam pulls a crumpled cloth from his pocket.)

TAM: Here. Let me bind 'at up fer ye.

ELLEN JEAN: Tis nothin', I said.

TAM: Garn. Ye musn 't be so stubborn.

              *(Tam takes her hand to wrap the bandage, then stops
              and stares at her webbed fingers. Ellen Jean pulls her
              hand away.)*

ELLEN JEAN: What are ye gleerin' at?

TAM: Yer hands, I . . . I niver saw the like o' them.

ELLEN JEAN: Then run and tell the others what ye've seen! Tell 'em
              ye've seen the webs. Tell 'em!

              (She angrily shoves her hands in his face.)

              Look! Green and slimy like seaweed, they are. They
              say she has horned skin on her palms. Tell 'em she
              goes doon tae the beach tae meet the King o' the Sea
              behind the rocks! Tell them! They'll think ye're a fine
              one fer knowin'.

              *(Ellen Jean turns to run away, but Tam catches her
              arm.)*

TAM: Wait! I'm sorry!

ELLEN JEAN: I hate ye, Tam McCodrun and all the others!

              (Ellen Jean breaks away and exits, running.)

TAM: *(Calling after her.)* Wait! I'm sorry! I said I'm sorry!
              Devil take ye, then.

              (Tam picks up his pail.)

              Devil take any who call me Dirty Tam! Devil take the
              limpets!

(Tam throws the tin pail into the rocks with a crash.)

Devil take the selkies!

(Tam looks after Ellen Jean. Quietly.) I didna mean it. I didna mean tae hurt ye.

LIGHTS SHIFT.

(Interior of the croft. Duncan kneels before the fire, brushing a selkie pelt with great tenderness. The sounds of the selkies can be heard in the distance. Pa stands outside the crofthouse watching Duncan.)

PA: Ye see, Duncan couldna destroy Margaret's pelt, or she would die. But he lived alus wi' the fear 'at she would discover it and return tae the sea. So he hid Margaret's skin careful-like aboot the croft, first in one place, then another, tae keep it from her searchin' eyes, oilin' and brushin' It each year so it wouldna crack or dry up. It was as though he was carin' fer Margaret herself.

(Pa enters the crofthouse and sits in the rocking chair, which squeaks noisily as he rocks back and forth. Pa opens his mouth as though to say something, then stops. Pa heaves a huge, audible sigh. Duncan looks at Pa sharply.)

PA: I didna say a word.

DUNCAN: Yer gettin' ready.

(Pa rocks furiously in the squeaky rocking chair.)

DUNCAN: Get on with it then.

PA: When I'm ready. When I'm ready.

DUNCAN: I'm in no rush.

(Pa rocks his chair with a vengeance to the rhythm of Duncan's brush strokes on the pelt.)

PA: Deer, Sheer, bret and smeer,
What shall ye have fer dinner?

(Duncan stops brushing and gives Pa an annoyed look. He begins his rhythmic brushing again.)

PA: Minch meat small or none at all,
Tae make ye fat or thinner.

DUNCAN: Ye'd best be ready soon, afore ye rock that chair intae the ground!

PA: Ye coulda had yer pick o' island lasses, fine and strong.

DUNCAN: Aye, 'ats the familiar tune.

PA: How could ye have done it, man? Ta'en one o' the selkie-folk tae wife?

DUNCAN: I didna choose it.

PA: And who forced ye?

DUNCAN: The first time I laid eyes on her sittin' on the skerrie, hair blowin' out around her like the mist, I knew I couldna rest 'til I brought her home tae wife.

PA: Now she canna rest. Walkin' doon tae the sea night after night. An' Ellen Jean, hidin' herself away on the croft, ashamed o' her hands.

DUNCAN: Things change. This year she'll be goin' doon tae the Foy with me tae dance.

PA: Ye'll be goin' alone tae the Foy this year. She's ta'en herself off tae bed.

DUNCAN: Tae bed? At this hour?

PA: She wilna dance at the Foy. She's afraid the others'll
            laugh. She canna find her place among the lads and
            lasses.

            (From the sea comes the sounds of the selkies.)

DUNCAN: *(Shouting to the selkies)* Leave off yer hoolan'. I canna
            think wi' the sound o' ye!

PA: The selkies're callin' tae Margaret, callin' her tae come
            away wi' 'em. Ye've grown careless. Best be hidin' her
            pelt away afore she comes back. If she finds her skin
            she'll be goin' back to the sea in a twinklin'.

DUNCAN: She wouldna leave me.

PA: She couldna help herself. It's inside her, like Ellen Jean
            swimmin' oot beyond the voe.

DUNCAN: No! She wouldna leave us, man, after fourteen years!

PA: Then why do ye no' give back her skin?

            (There is a moment of silence.)

            There's trouble in what ye've done. Ye canna run from a
            wrong.

DUNCAN: Are ye through?

PA: It's the bairns that pay fer the wrongs o' the ones gone
            afore. Ellen Jean'll be livin' wi' yer sin fer the rest o' her
            life. I shoulda beat ye wi' a stick 'til ye came to yer
            senses afore I let ye take yer wife from the sea.

DUNCAN: Ye shouldna blame yerself.

PA: I didna stop ye, noo, did I?   'At's me own wrong.

               *(Pa exits. The sound of the selkies calling grows louder
               and more plaintive. Duncan raises his fists in anger. He
               folds up the pelt and shoves it back into its hiding place
               above the aisins.)*

DUNCAN: *(Shouting out the door toward the sea.)* Be off noo!
               Stop yer callin'!

               *(Duncan slams the window shutters closed as though to
               lock out the sound. The moaning of the selkies grows
               even louder. Duncan opens the door and yells into the
               night.)*

               Go back tae the sea an' leave us alone. She belongs
               tae me. Do ye hear? She belongs tae me!

               *(Duncan slams the door and exits. The sound of the
               selkies continues to fill the crofthouse. Within their
               moaning sounds can be heard the sound of the selkies
               calling Ellen Jean's name. Ellen Jean enters, rubbing
               her eyes. She is wearing a white night dress and her
               hair hangs long down her back. She hugs herself and
               closing her eyes, sways in response to the selkie
               sounds. She opens the door and the selkie sounds grow
               louder. Her body moves instinctively to the sounds. As
               though directed to do so, Ellen Jean looks in the direc-
               tion of the pelt. She tries to reach it but it is too high.
               She drags over a stool and stands on it. Ellen Jean lifts
               the pelt down from its hiding place and hugs it to her
               body. She closes her eyes, and swaying back and forth,
               imitates the selkies' moaning with her own voice. She
               loses her balance and falls off the stool onto the floor
               with a crash. The selkie sounds stop. Pa enters.)*

PA: Ach, Jean! I thought it was the bawkie man come tae
               steal us away'. What're ye aboot?

ELLEN JEAN: Look. A selkie skin. I found it hidden up in the aisins.

PA: What're ye doin' searchin' up in the aisins?

ELLEN JEAN: The selkies woke me. Did ye no' hear 'em?

PA: Ye'd have to be stone deaf or dead no' tae hear their
              bellowin'.

ELLEN JEAN: No. No. The selkies were callin' me, callin' me name
              over and over.

PA: Selkies talkin'. What a bulder o' nonsense!

ELLEN JEAN: Clear as the broonie lights, they'us callin' me name. It
              was they made me look up in th' aisins. They wanted
              me tae find the pelt.

PA: Ye're dreamin', Jean. And walkin' in yer sleep by the
              look o' ye.

ELLEN JEAN: This selkie pelt is no' a dream. Maybe it belongs tae one
              o' the selkie-folk . . . like in the stories.

PA: More likely stuffed up there tae keep oot the drafty air.

ELLEN JEAN: Oh, Pa, think o' the poor creature withoot its skin.

PA: Long dead noo. They canno' live withoot their skins.

ELLEN JEAN: But it feels warm. Not like somethin' dead at all. I'll be
              goin' doon tae the sea.

PA: I'd think atifer doin' 'at, if I were thee. It's trouble ye're
              askin' fer. Return the pelt tae where ye found it. It
              doesna belong tae ye noo, does it?

ELLEN JEAN: No.

PA: Then ye're no' tae be takin' it.

                  (Ellen Jean lays the pelt against her cheek and breathes in the smell.)

ELLEN JEAN: There's somethin' aboot the smell.

                  (Ellen Jean holds out the pelt to Pa's nose.)

PA: *(Making a face.)* I'll no' be smellin' any old selkie skin!

ELLEN JEAN: I know the smell. It's . . . familiar.

PA: Ach, ye know the smell o' the sea, like all the Orkney folk.

ELLEN JEAN: I was meant tae find it, Pa. I know it.

PA: Ye were meant tae dance at the Johnsmas Foy, but ye're no' doin' it, then, are ye?

                  (Ellen Jean is silent.)

                  Come tae the Foy an' dance the music tae life with yer old Pa. Give the others a chance tae know who ye are inside.

ELLEN JEAN: I canno' dance fer the others. I canno'.

PA: And I canno' force ye tae dance. Sha' me the pelt and I'll return it tae where ye found it.

                  (Ellen Jean sighs and gives Pa the pelt. He puts it back up in the aisins.)

ELLEN JEAN: I'll ask Mither. She'll know what tae do aboot the pelt.

PA: No! Dunna be botherin' yer mither. Listen tae yer old Pa. Ferget ye ever saw the pelt.

ELLEN JEAN: But Pa, the selkies . . . they'us callin' me.

PA: *(Sharply)* 'Twas a dream, I tell ye. Ferget it, and dunna
               be borrowin' trouble. Things're likely tae be lookin'
               different in the mornin'.

               (Ellen Jean hesitates.)

               Go on with ye, I said.

               (Ellen Jean goes toward the door.)

               Ellen Jean.

               (Ellen Jean turns back to Pa.)

               Dunna be muckin' aboot with what ye dunna understand
               and canno' finish, do ye hear me?

ELLEN JEAN: Aye, I hear ye, Pa.

PA: Sleep well.

               (Exit Ellen Jean. The selkie sounds begin again.)

PA: Sleep well! That's no' likely, fer none this night.

               *(Exit Pa. Ellen Jean peeks around the doorway and
               sees Pa has gone. She enters and takes the pelt from
               its hiding place. The sounds of the selkies calling fills
               the room. Ellen Jean hugs herself and sways as if in
               ecstasy. Then she tucks the pelt under her arm and
               exits into the night.)*

               LIGHTS SHIFT. MUSIC.

               *(The beach. Dim light. Music fades. Sounds of the sea
               and the wind. Ellen Jean sits at center, looking out to
               sea. She wraps herself in the pelt, sways to and fro and*

smiles. For the first time, she seems happy and at peace. Sounds of the selkies approaching. Ellen Jean tries to fit herself into the pelt. She tries to put her foot into it, while her arms, attempting several styles of drapery, cannot quite manage to decipher its mystery. Enter the two selkie sisters, Red Hair and Black Hair. The two selkies glide in the sea toward the shore. Ellen Jean sees their approach and, frustrated by her inability to wear the pelt, folds herself as small as she can, hiding herself beneath it. The selkies haul out on the beach and cautiously move nearer to Ellen Jean. Enter Tam from behind the rocks, carrying a club. Tam wears the same dirty trousers, dingy white shirt and vest. He is barefoot. He sees Ellen Jean and the two selkies, and runs toward them, lifting the club high over his head to strike. The selkies bellow and escape into the sea. Ellen Jean jumps up and sees Tam about to hit her.)

ELLEN JEAN: No! Dunna strike me!

TAM: *(Jumping up in shock and dropping the club.)* Selkie Lass!

(Tam loses his footing on the slippery rocks.)

Help me! Help!

(Tam falls into the water and lies still.)

ELLEN JEAN: *(Calling after him.)* I hope ye drown. Ye deserve tae drown. Then no more selkies will die from the likes o' Dirty Tam McCodrun!

(When there is no answer, Ellen Jean looks down into the water.)

Why dunna ye swim? Afraid they'll say ye've a bit o' the selkie in ye? I hope ye go straight doon tae . . .

(The selkies bellow and yelp again.)

ELLEN JEAN: *(Realizing)* Giddy God! He's drownin'!

(Ellen Jean, leaving the pelt behind on the rock, enters the water. She moves to Tam, floating on the surface as if dead. Ellen Jean drags Tam onto the beach, with help from the two selkies.)

I'm sorry. I didna mean what I said. I dinna want ye tae die!

(Selkie music. Ellen Jean looks up and sees the two selkies behind her throw off their pelts. They are transformed into the two beautiful women seen with Margaret at the beginning of the play. Throughout the scene, the two selkies move in tandem as though connected.)

Giddy God!

BLACK HAIR:: Hush yer cryin'. He will no' die.

RED HAIR:: Ye have saved him this night. 'Tis the way o' the selkies tae save drownin' men, even the killers.

BLACK HAIR: He'll wake soon enough with an achin' head.

RED HAIR: None the worse fer the baffin.

ELLEN JEAN: I knowed ye would come when I saw ye oot on the skerrie.

RED HAIR: Ye found the pelt.

ELLEN JEAN: I heard ye callin' me. Tellin' me tae bring it.

BLACK HAIR: Ye have the ears tae listen this night and the heart tae tell ye what tae listen fer.

RED HAIR: Aye, and look. She has her Mither's eyes.

BLACK HAIR: Green as the sea.

ELLEN JEAN: Do ye know Mither?

BLACK HAIR: Aye, as we know the flow o' the tides and the feel o' the
               warm sun.

RED HAIR: Ye're very like her, yer mither.

BLACK HAIR: Sha' me yer hands.

               *(Black Hair takes Ellen Jean's hand and lifts back the
               long sleeves. Ellen Jean pulls her hands away and hides
               them both behind her back.)*

ELLEN JEAN: They're ugly.

               *(Black Hair takes Ellen Jean's hands in her own and
               caresses them.)*

BLACK HAIR: They are webbed.

RED HAIR: Made fer the sea.

               (Red Hair embraces Ellen Jean.)

ELLEN JEAN: *(To Red Hair)* Dunna be afraid. I'll keep ye safe. No
               hunters will find ye.

BLACK HAIR: She weeps fer one ta'en by a crofter fourteen years ago
               an' kept from her home an' family in th' sea.

ELLEN JEAN: Like in the stories.

BLACK HAIR: Tis no story. Tis true as ye're standin' there. The pelt
               belongs tae yer mither, our sister.

ELLEN JEAN: Mither? But she canno be one o' the selkie folk.
              She's . . . old.

BLACK HAIR: Fourteen years kept from the sea has made her old.

RED HAIR: Every year at Midsummer, we return tae be wi' her.
              Seven children she has in the sea, a fither, mither and
              we two sisters.

              *(Ellen Jean pulls back her sleeves and looks with new
              eyes at her webbed hands.)*

ELLEN JEAN: I'm one o' the selkie folk.

BLACK HAIR: No, lass. Yer part o' yer mither and part o' yer fither.
              Sea and land. The first of a kind.

ELLEN JEAN: *(Taking up the pelt and holding it close.)* I hate the land.
              I'm different from the others. I want tae be in the sea.

BLACK HAIR: Yer Mither belongs in the sea, but it is no' yer home.

ELLEN JEAN: I have no home. I dunna belong anywhere!

BLACK HAIR: Belongin's no' a place, it's inside ye. Ye will find the
              knowin', in time.

ELLEN JEAN: More waitin', alus waitin'. I canno' wait any longer.

RED HAIR: Ye must give yer mither back her pelt.

BLACK HAIR: So she can return tae her home in th' sea.

ELLEN JEAN: Return tae the sea? But will she come back?

              (Tam begins to stir. He coughs.)

BLACK HAIR: He's wakin'

RED HAIR: Quickly! The sea!

(Black Hair and Red Hair run to grab their pelts.)

ELLEN JEAN: Wait! If I give Mither the pelt, will she come back tae
                me? I need tae know!

BLACK HAIR: Give her the pelt!

RED HAIR: Give her back tae the sea!

                *(Black Hair and Red Hair throw on their pelts, and,
                entering the sea, are transformed into selkies. They
                swim away from shore and exit. Ellen Jean stands
                looking out to sea, watching the selkies. Tam sits up,
                sees her and smiles, then lies back down before she
                sees him awake. Ellen Jean goes to Tam, who moans
                loudly.)*

ELLEN JEAN: Please. Wake up. I didna mean fer ye tae die, just no'
                tae hurt me.

                *(Tam's arms go around her. He pulls her to him and
                kisses her.)*

ELLEN JEAN: *(Jumping up)* Oh!

TAM: *(Laughing)* A kiss from the Selkie Lass. Almost worth
                drownin' fer.

ELLEN JEAN: I hate ye, Tam McCodrun.

TAM: What? Fer a kiss?

ELLEN JEAN: Ye tried tae kill me. Again.

TAM: No. I was after the pelt. How was I tae know ye were
                darned doon in it?

ELLEN JEAN: Killin' was all ye were after. What kind o' man would club an innocent selkie?

TAM: The hungry kind.

ELLEN JEAN: The night of the Johnsmas Foy? There'll be plenty tae eat.

TAM: There's other kinds o' hunger than in the stomach.

ELLEN JEAN: What other kinds?

TAM: Did ye niver feel fairly silted tae have somethin', wantin' it so much ye can think o' naught but that?

ELLEN JEAN: Waitin' fer it tae happen, deathly afraid it niver will?

TAM: Aye, that's the feelin'.

ELLEN JEAN: What are ye silted fer?

TAM: Tae wake up every dawn in the same place. Tae have a place tae call home.

ELLEN JEAN: A place tae belong?

TAM: Aye, 'at's it. Even the feast at the Foy canno' fill up 'at yawnin' hole.

ELLEN JEAN: I know. I want tae belong, too.

TAM: Ye have a home. A fine croft wi' a byre full o' sheep and ponies, too.

ELLEN JEAN: What guid is it if none o' the others wants tae be with me?

TAM: I do.

ELLEN JEAN: Ye do?

TAM: Aye.

ELLEN JEAN: But ye're alus callin' me names and sayin' 'at hateful
               rhyme.

TAM: Ach, it's fer the lads. There's no meanin' in it.   I'll no' be
               makin' sport o' ye ever again, if ye ask me.

ELLEN JEAN: Why should I believe ye?

TAM: Ye saved me miserable life, did ye no'?

ELLEN JEAN: Aye, more's the pity.

TAM: Ask me, then.

ELLEN JEAN: I'm askin' ye. Dunna be callin' me names.

TAM: Niver again.

ELLEN JEAN: Swear it tae me.

TAM: I swear I'll niver call ye names again.

ELLEN JEAN: And ye'll no' be sayin' 'at hateful rhyme?

TAM: I swear I'll no' say that rhyme ever again.

ELLEN JEAN: And swear tae me from this day on ye'll niver raise a
               hand tae hurt the selkies as long as ye live.

TAM: I've done enough swearin' fer one day.

ELLEN JEAN: Please. 'Tis all I'm askin' fer.

TAM: Do ye know the price 'ats paid oot fer a single selkie
               pelt?

ELLEN JEAN: There's other ways tae earn yer keep.

TAM: I'm savin' up fer somethin'.

ELLEN JEAN: What're ye savin' up fer, Tam McCodrun?

(Tam looks at her sharply, realizing she has said his name with respect.)

TAM: *(Eagerly)* A bit o' land - a home. A lass tae love me as brave and true as yerself.

ELLEN JEAN: Are ye sayin' 'at because I saved yer miserable life?

TAM: Better ye let me die.

ELLEN JEAN: Niver say such a thing. It might come true. Did yer mither never tell ye?

TAM: She's long dead. The day I wus born.

ELLEN JEAN: I'm sorry. I canno' imagine a life withoot Mither.

TAM: Ach, who wants all that fussin' over.

(Tam sighs and takes up the pelt.)

I'll content meself wi' this spotty pelt.

ELLEN JEAN: No. It belongs tae me.

TAM: I can take this pelt if I want. Ye canno' stop me. And maybe if I keep it, ye'll follow me.

ELLEN JEAN: I'll no' follow a thief. The pelt belongs tae me. Ye canno' have it.

TAM: I'll no' take yer pelt . . . if ye'll dance with me at the Foy this night.

ELLEN JEAN: Ye want tae dance wi' me? At the Foy?

TAM: Aye, that's the trade. The pelt fer a dance.

ELLEN JEAN: Dance at the Foy! Aye, I'll dance with ye!

               (Suddenly shy) If that's what ye want.

TAM: I said it, did I no'?

ELLEN JEAN: Will ye promise no' tae harm the selkies?

TAM: It's a hard bargain yer askin' fer, Lass.

ELLEN JEAN: Aye.

TAM: Aye.

ELLEN JEAN: Done?

TAM: Done.

               *(Tam hands Ellen Jean the pelt and she rolls it into a
               bundle.)*

ELLEN JEAN: I have somethin' important tae do. Be off with ye noo.

TAM: What's makin' ye so foreswifted tae be rid o' me?

ELLEN JEAN: I have somethin' tae do before the Foy. Get on with ye.

TAM: Ye're mighty mysterious. What're ye aboot?

ELLEN JEAN: *(Casting about for an excuse.)* Oh. Well, I canno' go tae
               the Foy in me nightdress, can I?

TAM: *(He looks down at his dirty hands and feet.)* Oh, I'm
               thinkin' I have somethin' tae do, too.

ELLEN JEAN: Dunna ferget yer promise.

TAM: I swear I'll no' hurt the selkies.

ELLEN JEAN: Ferever, no matter what comes.

TAM: I said it, did I no'?

ELLEN JEAN: *(Taking hold of his arms.)* Say it.

TAM: Ferever, no matter what comes.

ELLEN JEAN: Niver - niver forget yer promise.

(Tam reaches out his hand and touches her.)

TAM: I'll no' ferget.

ELLEN JEAN: Run. Dunna come back until Midnight! Until the Foy!

TAM: Until the Foy!

*(Giving a joyous shout, Tam turns and runs offstage.
Ellen Jean looks up and down the beach, then dances
around the beach whirling and high stepping with joy.
As she dances, Margaret enters, and quietly watches
her daughter.)*

ELLEN JEAN: I'll dance - dance at the Foy! And be one o' them!

(Panting, Ellen Jean hugs herself with pleasure.)

MARGARET: Tis guid tae see ye smilin', Peedie Buddo.

ELLEN JEAN: Mither!

*(Ellen Jean runs to her mother, throws her arms around
her mother's waist and holds her.)*

ELLEN JEAN: Oh, Mither, I'm goin' tae dance at the Foy - with Tam!

MARGARET: A smart lad, that Tam. And lucky, too.

ELLEN JEAN: And . . . and look . . . I found yer pelt.

MARGARET: Ahhhh. Me pelt! Ye found me pelt!

(Laughing, Margaret falls to her knees on the beach, caressing the pelt and breathing in the familiar smell.)

ELLEN JEAN: Mither, ye're laughin'.

MARGARET: Oh, Peedie Buddo, ye 've given me back me life.

ELLEN JEAN: Yer sisters said ye'll leave me fer the sea.

MARGARET: Leave ye? No, Peedie Buddo. I'll alus be with ye. Come.

(Margaret holds out her hand and Ellen Jean takes it in her own. Margaret leads Ellen Jean down to the sea.)

MARGARET: Fourteen years I have been captive on the land. In that time I have grown old and stiff. Me skin is dry and cracked fer want o' the sea. Me bones are as brittle as driftwood lyin' on the shore. Ye have brought me what I need. It is me time tae return home.

(Margaret folds her arms around Ellen Jean and holds her.)

ELLEN JEAN: Mither, please, dunna leave me!

(The sound of the wind and the sea.)

MARGARET: I will alus be with ye. Look tae the sea and ye'll see me there. In the waves breakin' on the shore, the sun glitterin' on the sea foam. Precious shells will wash up on the beach. Fish will leap intae yer nets and the selkies will guide ye safely through the tides in the sea.

(Margaret kisses Ellen Jean on each cheek.)

ELLEN JEAN: No! Mither! Take me with ye! I want tae go with ye!

MARGARET: Are ye no' afraid?

ELLEN JEAN: Aye. Afraid o' bein' left behind among the others.

MARGARET: Listen well then, Peedie Buddo. I give ye the gift o' the wind tae travel beneath the tides. Only do as I do and ye will have the way tae find the knowin'.

(Music. Ellen Jean follows her mother's lead as she dances the journey beneath the sea and, in a rhythmic exchange of breath, bestows the gift of the wind upon her daughter.)

MARGARET: Me heart is turned inside oot with the pain o' leavin' ye, but it is me time tae go.

(Margaret turns and walks into the sea with the pelt. She puts it around her body and is transformed into a selkie. She glides swiftly into the sea and, without turning back, exits. Ellen Jean runs onto the rock at center.)

ELLEN JEAN: Wait! Wait fer me! Dunna leave me behind!

(Music from the Foy can be heard in the background. Enter Pa.)

PA: Ellen Jean. Hover thee, Lass. Ye canno' follow her. Stay and dance fer yer old Pa at the Foy.

(Sounds of the selkies calling. Ellen Jean looks toward the sea.)

ELLEN JEAN: Can ye no' hear 'em callin' me? I canno' stay on land.

PA: But the tides, Jean.

ELLEN JEAN: Dunna be afraid fer me, Pa. I'll find it. I'll find the knowin'.

PA: Jean, I canno' let ye go.

ELLEN JEAN: Dunna try tae stop me. If ye hold me here I'll hate ye ferever. *(Pa embraces Ellen Jean.)*

PA: Go then and St. Magnus be wi' ye. Quickly! Duncan's comin' fer the Foy.

ELLEN JEAN: I love ye, Pa.

(Enter Tam. He wears the same dirty clothes, but his face, hands and bare feet are clean and his hair is combed and tied back neatly. He carries a bunch of heather.)

TAM: Selkie Lass! I've come fer me dance! Listen! They're comin' up the beach fer the Foy!

(Ellen Jean looks toward Tam, then toward the sea.)

ELLEN JEAN: Dunna ferget yer promise, Tam McCodrun! Dunna ever ferget!

(The sound of the wind increases. Ellen Jean runs to the water's edge and enters the sea. She swiftly follows the path her mother has taken. Tam runs forward onto the rock.)

TAM: No! Wait! Ye promised me a dance!

(Exit Ellen Jean.)

TAM: Come back! Come Back! Ye'll drown!

            (Sounds of the wind as though a storm is approaching.
            Tam removes his vest, and prepares to leap into the sea
            to save Ellen Jean.)

PA: Hover thee, Lad.

TAM: I've got tae find her!

PA: Ye canno' swim.

TAM: I canno' stand here like a fool and do nuthin'.

PA: There's naught tae be done fer it. Drownin' yerself oot
            there wilna bring her back. She's gone. She heard the
            selkies callin' her. It was her time, just as it was her
            mither's time tae go.

TAM: God fergive me! I made sport o' her.

PA: There, Lad, tis none o' yer doin'. It's no' yer fault.

TAM: But why did she run from me?

PA: Twas no' a runnin' from, Lad, but runnin' to. Ach, ye'd
            no' believe me if I told ye.

TAM: I want tae know.

PA: (Struggling to find the words to explain.) Sometimes ye
            have tae lose somethin' terrible dear tae gain what ye
            want most.

TAM: I dunna understand.

PA: Might do me some guid tae tell ye all o' it. Ye'll stay this
            night at the crofthouse. With a roof over yer head and a
            fire warmin' me bones, I'll tell ye the tale. Perhaps we
            need each other.

(The music of the Foy rises in the distance. The sound of the wind howling and the sea waves crashing.)

TAM: *(Looking toward the music.)* What will we tell the others at the Foy?

PA: We'll tell 'em a wrong was done afore ye were born. And this is the price tae be paid oot fer it.

TAM: *(Looking towards the sea.)* Will she come back?

PA: *(Crossing himself.)* Only St. Magnus knows, Lad. But if she does return, she'll have a knowin' beyond all the others.

LIGHTS SHIFT. SELKIE SOUNDS. MUSIC.

(Black Hair, Red Hair and the selkie Margaret, wearing their pelts, enter the sea area, doing a version of the dance seen at the beginning of the play that suggests the denser movement beneath the sea. They are celebrating Margaret's return home.)

DUNCAN: *(Offstage voice, calling from a distance.)* Margaret!

(Margaret responds to the sound of Duncan's voice then slowly returns to the dance. With each sound of Duncan's call, she reacts less and less until she is deaf to his cries.)

Margaret! Margaret! Come back! Margaret!

(Margaret and the two selkie sisters exit. Duncan enters, running.)

Margaret! Margaret!

(Duncan collapses onto the rocks.)

LIGHTS SHIFT.

(Dim light. The beach. One year later. Midsummer's Eve, the night of the Johnsmas Foy. Sounds of the wind and the sea. At center sits Tam, looking out to sea. He wears clean trousers, a shirt and a new colorful vest. His hair is combed neatly. Fiddle music. Pa enters, carrying his fiddle.)

PA: *(To the audience.)* Listen. Can ye no' hear the music? (He listens.) A year has passed. It's Midsummer's Eve, the night o' the Johnsmas Foy, one year ago since our Ellen Jean was lost tae the sea. It's nearly midnight. Soon the torches'll be lit and the dancin' on the beach'll last til the cock crows. It'll be a guid harvest this year. Plenty tae eat fer everyone, rich and poor alike. But there's some hunger canno' be satisfied wi' food, no matter how rich and fine.

(The sound of the selkies singing.)

TAM: Pa, look! There's selkies swimmin' in.

PA: Aye. Like alus they come back at Midsummer's Eve.

TAM: How do they know it's Midsummer's Eve?

PA: The light. The tides. The heat in the air. It's in their blood.

TAM: Do ye think they know aboot Ellen Jean?

PA: *(Crosses himself.)* Only St. Magnus knows, Lad.

TAM: There's somethin' aboot Midsummer. It alus feels like the beginnin' o' things.

PA: Tis a beginnin'. Yer a fine one noo, ye are, workin' yer own bit o' land.

TAM: Thanks tae yer kindness.

PA: What a bulder o' nonsense! Ye earned the land wi' hard
                   work. Ye're like me own family, Lad.

                   *(Enter Duncan, disheveled and dressed in rags as
                   though he can no longer care for himself.)*

DUNCAN: There she is! 'Tis Ellen Jean comin' up the beach.

PA: No, no, Duncan, that's the others comin' fer the Foy.

DUNCAN: I see her. She's comin'. She's put on her bonnie dress
                   and Margaret's done up her hair with ribbons. Jean!

PA: No, Duncan. Ellen Jean's drowned followin' her mither
                   oot tae sea. Ye know that, man.

                   (Duncan hangs his head and moans.)

DUNCAN: She'll come. She'll come tae dance.

PA: *(To Tam)* Poor guid man. He wilna give up hopin' she'll
                   come back.

TAM: Aye. Waitin' each day on the beach fer her.

PA: He's near lost his mind wi' the sorrow.

DUNCAN: Jean! Jean! She's comin'. She's only waitin' fer the
                   torches tae be lit and the music tae start. Pa! Play yer
                   fiddle. Then Ellen Jean'll dance!

TAM: *(To Duncan)* Sir, come wi' me tae the crofthouse. We'll
                   pour ye some ale and sit ye by the fire.

DUNCAN: Play yer fiddle, Pa! Play and she'll come. She's only
                   waitin' tae hear the music.

(Shaking his head, Pa takes up his fiddle and plays a tune. Duncan goes round the beach lighting the torches of heather. When the torches are lit, Pa ends the music.)

DUNCAN: Where is she? Where's me daughter? Where's Ellen Jean? Margaret, give her back tae me! I canna undo what I have done. Give me back me daughter!

(Duncan falls to his knees on the beach. Selkie music. Ellen Jean rises from behind the rocks at the side of the stage, bathed in golden light. Her nightdress is changed to shimmering luminescent material the color of the sea, with sleeves short enough to reveal her hands.)

ELLEN JEAN: Tam! Tam McCodrun. I've come fer me dance.

TAM: Giddy God! Ellen Jean!

DUNCAN: Jean! Me own darlin' daughter! Ye've come back!

(Duncan runs to Ellen Jean and throws his arms around her.)

I thought ye were lost, lost tae the sea ferever.

ELLEN JEAN: Lost? No, I am found. I've been tae the bottom o' the sea. Mither breathed intae me the wind tae travel beneath the tides. I have known the selkie-folk, me other family. Seven fine brothers and sisters I have below.

DUNCAN: And yer Mither?

ELLEN JEAN: She fergives ye.

DUNCAN: Will she come back tae me?

ELLEN JEAN: She will alus be with ye. Look tae the sea. If ye're hungry, the fishes will leap intae yer nets. Precious shells will wash up on the beach. Yer boat will glide safely through the tides in the ocean and the rocks on the shore. Mither will be yer guide.

DUNCAN: Jean, Jean, I knew ye'd come back.

(Ellen Jean goes to her Grandpa and kisses him.)

ELLEN JEAN: The waitin' is over, Pa. I've found the knowin'.

PA: Dance, Ellen Jean! Dance the stories tae life!

(The music of the Foy swells.)

ELLEN JEAN: Have ye kept yer promise, Tam McCodrun?

TAM: Aye, I said it, did I no'? Will ye be keepin' yers?

ELLEN JEAN: I choose tae dance. I'm fairly silted tae dance wi' ye, Tam!

(Ellen Jean holds out her hand to Tam. Tam takes her hand. They look to Pa. Pa takes up his fiddle and begins to play. Tam and Ellen Jean do a version of the dance done by Ellen Jean earlier in the play, Tam following Ellen Jean's lead. As they dance, Duncan fades offstage. As the lights dim, Pa ends the tune and walks downstage.)

PA: And so it was tha' the sea married the land. And in the union the island folk saw the birth o' a new kind o' folk - called the clan McCodrun. Across the islands their stories o' the sea and the land can be heard round the peat fires and the Johnsmas Foy is the merrier fer their dancin'. And on Midsummer's Eve, the seventh tide o' the seventh tide, the spirit o' Ellen Jean can still be seen sittin' on the skerrie, whisperin' softlike tae one beautiful, brown-spotted selkie with eyes green as the sea. And

tae this day if ye come tae Orkney ye might see a lad or
lass with the webbed hands. Dunna be surprised.
They're the children o' the children o' the children o' the
traveller Tam and Ellen Jean, the Selkie Lass.

FIDDLE MUSIC. LIGHTS FADE TO BLACKOUT.

THE END

GLOSSARY

aisins - the eaves of a house, esp. the angular space between the top of the sidewall and the roof.

baffin - a severe drenching or dunking

bairn - a child

ballin' - throwing or pitching

bannock - a round, flat, griddle-baked bread, made of oat or barley meal

Bawkie Man - boogie man

bonny - pretty

buy buy - Orcadian expression (tsk, tsk)

byre - barn

croft - a farm by the sea

crofthouse - a farmhouse with attached barn

crofter - farmer

daive - to stupefy with a continued noise

darn - to conceal or hide

foreswifted - in a hurry

foy - celebration, party, feast

gully - a knife used for cutting fish

guid - good

har - dense fog

hover - to pause, wait a little

Hoy - one of the Orkney Islands

ill-bisted - testy, cross

kelp - seaweed

Kirkwall - largest town in Orkney

limpets - a kind of shellfish

Midsummer - June 21st, the first day of summer

peat - compressed earth used for fuel

peedie - little, small

Peedie Buddo - a term of endearment

selkie - the common or grey seal

selkie folk - selkies said to take human form on the land

sha me - give me

silted - to hunger exceedingly

skelly - adjective of the sky when it is covered by bright, glittering clouds

skerrie - a rock covered by sea at high tide

skirly-wheeter - a bit of skirt, an attractive girl

St. Magnus - patron saint of Orkney
Stromness - an Orcadian town, second largest to Kirkwall
stunder - a whim or impulsive decision
Tam - Orcadian pronunciation for Tom
voe - a protected inlet

All definitions adapted from The Orkney Norn: A Dictionary, History and
Etymology of the Orcadian Dialect by Hugh Marwick, The Oxford University Press, 1929.

NOTES FROM THE PLAYWRIGHT:

A reliable source for sounds of the grey and common seals is BBC Radio Orkney, Castle Street, Kirkwall, Orkney, KW15-IDF, telephone 001-44-1856-87-3939. Information regarding original Orcadian fiddle music is also available from this source.

The music in the play has three parts: the lively fiddle music played by Pa, the magical music of the selkies, which may include sounds of the sea, the wind and the selkies moaning, and finally, the fiddle music of the Johnsmas Foy.

Song, *Listen to the Sea*, Music by Elliot Sokolov, Lyrics by Laurie Brooks Gollobin, Copyright 1996, music used by permission of User Friendly Music (BMI).

The dialect is written to suggest the archaic, musical language called the Orkney Norn. It is spoken gently, suggested rather than affected. The r's are rolled softly, ing becomes in', you becomes ye (pronounced yuh). To becomes tae, pronounced "tay". The consonent "s", when ending a word, becomes a soft sh sound. Peedie Buddo is pronounced with a long ee in peedie and the oo sound in buddo. Aisins is pronounced with the dipthong ae. The expression Giddy (as in Giddy God!), mither, and fither are all pronounced with the short i sound. All other words are pronounced as they are spelled. See glossary at end of play for Orkney word definitions.

The Orcadian culture is a unique blending of the characteristics of early Norse settlers and later Scottish influence. Therefore, the dancing should not be an imitation of typical Scottish dances such as the High-land Fling. The dancing may contain hints of the Scottish culture, but is best choreographed imaginatively to reflect the movement and beauty of the sea so central to the world of the play.

These traditional Orcadian rhymes are taken from children's games:

Eetam, peetam, penny pie,
Pop-a-larum, jinkum jie,
Stand thoo there 'til I come by.

I warn ye once, I warn ye twice,
I warn ye oot the glowne's eyes.

Deer, sheer, bret and smeer,
What shall ye have fer dinner?
Minch meat small or none at all,
Tae make ye fat or thinner.

The author would like to warmly acknowledge and thank the following for their assistance in bringing Selkie to life:

In Orkney - The Zawadski Family of Balfour Castle, Sandy Firth, Robert Leslie, Carole Fathergill and the Shapinsay school, Mike Wallace of BBC Radio Orkney, and the Kirkwall Library.

In the United States - The Marine Mammal Commission of Washington, DC, Amie Brockway and The Open Eye Theatre, Doroth Webb and The Bonderman/IUPUI Symposium, The Kennedy Center's New Visions/New Voices, Alan Levy and The Hartford Children's Theatre, Lowell and Nancy Swortzell and The Program in Educational Theatre at New York University, Max Bush, Lauren Friesen, my patient and loving family, and always, Aurand Harris.

Selkie was a winner of the Sixth National Waldo M. and Grace C. Bonderman Youth Theatre Playwriting Workshop sponsored by Indiana University-Purdue University at Indianapolis and was featured in a rehearsed reading at the 1995 Youth Theatre Playwriting Symposium held in Indianapolis.

Selkie was also featured in a rehearsed reading at the 1995 New Visions/New Voices New Play Development Symposium at the John F. Kennedy Center in Washington, DC, with the New York University Program in Educational Theatre as producing organization, directed by Nancy Swortzell.

LISTEN TAE THE SEA

"SELKIE"

Music by Elliot Sokolov * Lyric by Laurie Brooks Gollobin
(c) 1996

Moderately slowly, with a sense of mystery

23
come a - long Beck - on ye tae sing the song. LIST - EN TAE THE
27
SEA THERE IS A LAND FAR BE - NEATH
30
A - WAK - EN FROM YURE SLEEP
32
TAE THE MYS - T'RIES DOON BE - LOW